# if...

## A Mind-Bending Way of Looking at Big Ideas and Numbers

Written by **David J. Smith** • Illustrated by **Steve Adams**

**WAYLAND**
www.waylandbooks.co.uk

The big numbers and data in this book are factual, as far as we know. But nobody knows exactly how old Earth is, or exactly how big the Universe is, or exactly how big Earth's population is, or when the first animals appeared or how many species there are. With really big numbers, there is lots of room for error. The data in this book is based on the most reliable estimates.

For teachers and colleagues who helped me to understand and appreciate our place in the Universe: Kathleen Raoul, Stan Sheldon, Mary Eliot, Ned Ryerson, Frederick S. Allis, Jack Schliemann, Bill Bellows, Anne McCormack, Jen Tobin, Jane Hardy and many others. And for the indomitable and endlessly supportive Val Wyatt. And always for Suzanne, my compass and my North Star. — D. J. S.

★

To Kaliane, Nick, Samantha, Stella-Rose and Victoria: Your little hands of today will do great things tomorrow! — S.A.

Text © 2014 David J. Smith
Illustrations © 2014 Steve Adams

Published in paperback in 2016 by Wayland

Published by permission of Kids Can Press Ltd., Toronto, Ontario, Canada

Dewey Number: 032'.02-dc23

ISBN: 978 0 7502 9384 6

Printed in China

10 9 8 7 6 5 4 3

Wayland
An imprint of Hachette Children's Group
Part of Hodder & Stoughton
Carmelite House
50 Victoria Embankment
London EC4Y 0DZ

An Hachette UK Company
www.hachette.co.uk
www.hachettechildrens.co.uk

# Contents

# iF...

How big is Earth or the Solar System or the Milky Way galaxy?
How old is our planet and when did the first animals and people appear on it?
Some things are so huge or so old that it's hard to wrap your mind around them.
But what if we took these big, hard-to-imagine objects and events and compared
them to things we can see, feel and touch? Instantly, we'd see our world in a
whole new way. That's what this book is about – it scales down, or shrinks,
huge events, spaces and times to something we can understand.
If you've had a doll or a model aeroplane, you know what scaling down means.
A scale model is a small version of a large thing. Every part is reduced
equally, so that you don't end up with a doll with enormous feet
or a model plane with giant wings.
And when we scale down some really huge things – such as the
Solar System or all of human history – some of the results are
quite surprising, as you are about to see...

# OUR GALAXY

iF the Milky Way galaxy was shrunk to the size of a dinner plate...

* our whole Solar System – the Sun and the planets – would be far smaller than this speck of dust, too small to see

* the visible Universe, on the other hand, would be about the size of Belgium.

The Hubble Space Telescope can see approximately 3000 galaxies. If each of these galaxies were represented by one dinner plate...

* there would be a stack of 3000 dinner plates about 115 metres (375 feet) tall, roughly the height of a 38-storey building.

In the whole Universe, there may be more than 170 billion (170 000 000 000) galaxies. If each one of these were a dinner plate...

* the stack would be about 6 720 000 kilometres (4 175 000 miles) high, 17 times the distance from Earth to the Moon.

When we measure distance in space, we use a measurement called a light year. A light year is the distance light travels in one year, and it's a huge distance – 9 460 800 000 000 km (5 865 696 000 000 miles).

Our Solar System is about 1/1000th of a light year from side to side.

The Milky Way galaxy is about 100 000 light years across.

The visible Universe is estimated to be approximately 92 billion (that's 92 000 000 000) light years across.

So the Universe is 920 000 times larger than the Milky Way galaxy, and the Milky Way is 100 million (100 000 000) times bigger than our Solar System.

# THE PLANETS

If the planets in the Solar System were shrunk to the size of balls and Earth was the size of a baseball...

* Mercury would be about the size of a table tennis ball
* Venus, a tennis ball
* Mars, a golf ball
* Jupiter, an exercise ball
* Saturn, a beach ball
* Uranus, a basketball
* Neptune, a football.

The Sun would be bigger than any ball, about 10 times the diameter of Jupiter.

8

Mercury

Venus

Earth

Mars

Jupiter

If the planets in the Solar System were laid out on a 100-metre American football field, and the Sun was the size of a grapefruit on one goal line...

* Mercury would be on the 4-metre line, Venus on the 7, Earth on the 10 and Mars on the 15. Each would be about the size of a grain of salt.

* Jupiter would be a large pea just beyond the midfield line and Saturn a smaller pea on the opposite goal line.

* Uranus and Neptune, each the size of a sesame seed, would be out of sight, far beyond the goal line.

Saturn

Uranus

Neptune

# HISTORY OF EARTH

iF the 4.5-billion-year history of Earth was compressed into a single year...

January February March April May June July August September October

iF the entire history of Earth from its very beginning was a two-hour DVD, humans would appear in the last second of the video.

* on 1 January, Earth forms

* around the middle of February, the Moon appears. In the third week of February, the oceans and atmosphere appear, as does the land mass that will eventually break up and become the continents.

* by the third week of March, the first life forms appear in the sea

* in April, more complex life forms appear in the sea

* towards the middle of June, oxygen is released into the atmosphere from algae and other microscopic life in the sea, paving the way for living things that breathe oxygen. In late June, the first great ice age occurs.

* in early November, another great ice age occurs and more complex life forms, such as small fish, arrive. From the end of November to the middle of December, many new kinds of life evolve and the first animals appear on land.

* around 18 December, the first birds emerge. Close to 22 December, mammals evolve. Near the last day of December, humans appear.

11

# LIFE ON EARTH

iF the 3.5 billion years of life on Earth were reduced to one hour...

* the first life forms — one-celled organisms such as bacteria — appear in the first second of the hour

* fish show up at 51 minutes and 10 seconds, and amphibians appear at 54 minutes, 10 seconds

* the dinosaurs arrive at 56 minutes and are gone 3 minutes later

* mammals appear at 56 minutes, 25 seconds

* the earliest birds appear at 58 minutes

* our earliest human ancestors finally make an appearance at 59 minutes, 56 seconds

* modern humans — the humans we are related to — show up at 59 minutes, 59.8 seconds.

**iF** the time frame was one day — 24 hours instead of 1 hour — then the first life forms appear just after midnight, fish at 8:28 p.m., the first mammals at 10:36 p.m. and our earliest human ancestors at about 24 minutes before midnight. Modern humans show up at 5 seconds before midnight, just as the day is ending.

# EVENTS OF THE LAST 3000

| Sunday | Monday | Tuesday | Wednesday |
|---|---|---|---|
| | **1** Use of iron becomes widespread. | **2** | **3** First Olympic Games are held (776 BCE). |
| **7** Alexander the Great builds a vast empire (336–323 BCE). | **8** Great Wall of China is built (221 BCE). | **9** | **10** Jesus Christ is born (5 BCE). |
| **14** | **15** The Middle Ages begin. | **16** Muhammad is born (570). | **17** |
| **21** William the Conqueror invades England and becomes king (1066). | **22** | **23** Genghis Khan becomes head of the Mongols (1206). | **24** The Black Death ravages Europe (1347–1350). |
| **28** The French Revolution begins (1789) and ends (1799). | **29** Alexander Graham Bell invents the telephone (1876). | **30** The first computer is built (1939). The Internet is created (1969). | **31** Evidence of water is discovered on Mars (2013). |

# YEARS

**If** the history of the last 3000 years was condensed into one month...

| Thursday | Friday | Saturday |
|---|---|---|
| **4** | **5** Buddha is born (560 BCE). Confucius is born (551 BCE). | **6** |
| **11** City of Pompeii is destroyed by Vesuvius eruption (79 CE). | **12** Paper is invented in China (105). | **13** |
| **18** Medicine and the sciences flourish in Arab Spain (around 750). | **19** | **20** Vikings are the first Europeans to reach North America (late 900s). |
| **25** Columbus reaches the Americas (1492). | **26** African slaves are first shipped to the Americas (1510). | **27** The dodo bird becomes extinct (1690). |

15

# INVENTIONS THROUGH TIME

**IF** all the inventions and discoveries humans have made were laid out along a measuring tape 100 cm (1 m) long...

At one end is the first human discovery – fire. People first used fire about 790 000 years ago to keep themselves warm and to cook their food.

About halfway along, humans first build shelters.

In the last 2.8 mm come all the inventions of the past 2000 years, everything from the number zero, to paper and plastics, telephones, cars, computers and satellites.

0 81 82 83 84 85 86 87 88 89 90 91 92 93 94 95 96 97 98 99 100

The bow and arrow is first used.

The wheel is invented.

Pottery is invented.

# INVENTIONS OF THE LAST

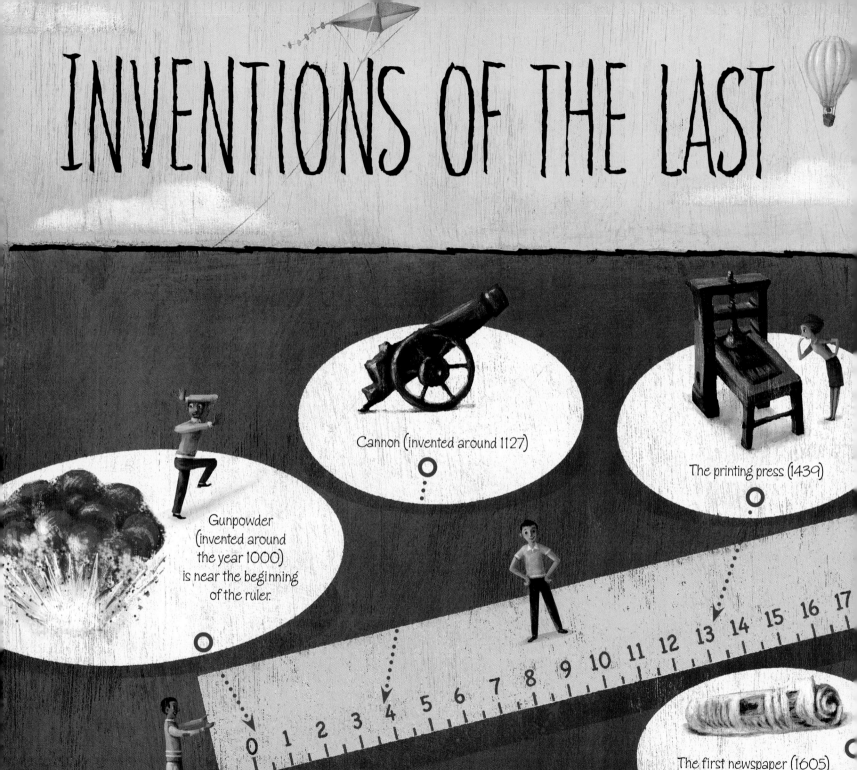

Gunpowder (invented around the year 1000) is near the beginning of the ruler.

Cannon (invented around 1127)

The printing press (1439)

The first newspaper (1605)

Glasses (1286)

# 1000 YEARS

iF the inventions of the last 1000 years were laid out along this ruler...

The railroad locomotive (1814)

The aeroplane, radio, television, computer, nuclear power, video games and many more inventions appear in the 20th century and the first years of the 21st century — the last 3.75 cm of the ruler.

19 20 21 22 23 24 25 26 27 28 29 30

The telephone (1876) and the light bulb (1880)

The Internet, DVDs, smartphones, tablets and other inventions we use today are at the very end of the ruler.

The thermometer (1724)

# THE CONTINENTS

iF the surface of Earth was shrunk to fit across two pages of this book...

* three-quarters would be in blue for the seas and oceans
* the remaining one-quarter would be in different colours for the continents:

  - Asia would take up about 7.5% of Earth's surface
  - Africa 5%
  - North America 4.1%
  - South America 3%
  - Antarctica 2.3%
  - Europe 1.7%
  - Oceania (Australia, New Zealand and the other islands of the Pacific) 1.4%.

Asia 7.5%

Africa 5%

South America 3%

Antarctica 2.3%

Europe 1.7%

Oceania 1.4%

North America 4.1%

# WATER

iF all the water
on Earth was
represented
by 100 glasses...

* 97 of the glasses would
   be filled with salt water
   from the oceans and some lakes

* 3 of the glasses would contain fresh
   water. One of these glasses would represent
   all the fresh water available to us. The rest of the
   fresh water is locked up in glaciers, frozen in
   the atmosphere or inaccessible deep underground.

Who uses the water and for what? We use about 10% of all the Earth's water in and around our homes — for drinking, cooking, washing and other household needs. People in North America use about 2 1/2 bathtubs of water per person a day for household purposes. In Europe, it's about 2 bathtubs full. In Africa, that number falls as low as 1/10 of a bathtub, even though the United Nations says that 1/4 bathtub of water per person is needed for health and well-being.

Household needs are small compared with water used in industry and agriculture. Industry uses twice as much water as households do — about 20% of all the world's water. And agriculture uses 70% of Earth's water. So the places that use the most water are the places that have the most water-intensive agriculture. Asia, in particular, is responsible for about 3/4 of the water use in the world.

# SPECIES OF LIVING THINGS

iF all species of living things on Earth were represented by a tree with 1000 leaves...

\* 753 leaves would be animals –
including every multi-celled animal,
from beetles to cats, to humans to whales

**TIC TOC**

How fast are species disappearing? Long ago, about one leaf disappeared from the tree every 1000 years. (One leaf represents 1750 known species.) However, today extinctions are happening at a faster rate, mainly because of habitat destruction and loss. As a result, some scientists predict that our tree with its 1000 leaves may lose as many as 200 leaves in the next 20 years or so. But new species are being discovered all the time, so new leaves are also being added to the tree.

* about 46 leaves would be protozoa – one-celled, animal-like organisms – and algae together

* 41 leaves would be fungi, such as mushrooms and yeast

* 154 leaves would be plants

* 6 leaves would be bacteria.

# MONEY

**IF** all the wealth in the world –
about 147 trillion (147 000 000 000 000)
pounds – was represented by a pile
of 100 coins...

* the richest 1% of the world's population
   would have 40 of the coins
* 9% would have 45 coins
* 40% would have 14 coins
* the poorest 50% – half the world's
   population – would share just one coin.

IF the 100 coins were divided among the continents, here's where they would be...

North America, 32 coins

Europe, 34 coins

Asia, 22 coins

Africa, 3 coins

South America, 6 coins

Oceania, 3 coins

# ENERGY

iF all the energy sources in the world were represented by 100 light bulbs...

---

* 2 light bulbs would be powered by hydroelectric power
* 6 by nuclear energy
* 11 by renewable energy — wind, geothermal and biomass
* 21 by gas
* 27 by coal
* 33 by oil.

In other words, fossil fuels (gas, coal and oil) would power 81 of the 100 light bulbs.

Hydroelectric 2%

Nuclear Energy 6%

Renewable Energy 11%

Gas 21%

Coal 27%

Oil 33%

iF all the world's energy consumption was a big chocolate bar with 12 squares...

* people in Asia and Oceania (Australia, New Zealand and the other islands of the Pacific) would consume 4 squares

* Europeans, 3

* North Americans, 3

* Africans, 1

* people in Central and South America, 1.

# LIFE EXPECTANCY

iF average life expectancy (the number of years people live) was represented by footprints in the sand...

* the average person would leave 70 steps because average life expectancy is 70 years. But that's an average. Not everyone leaves 70 steps.

* South Americans, 74

* Asians, 70 steps

* Africans would leave 58 steps

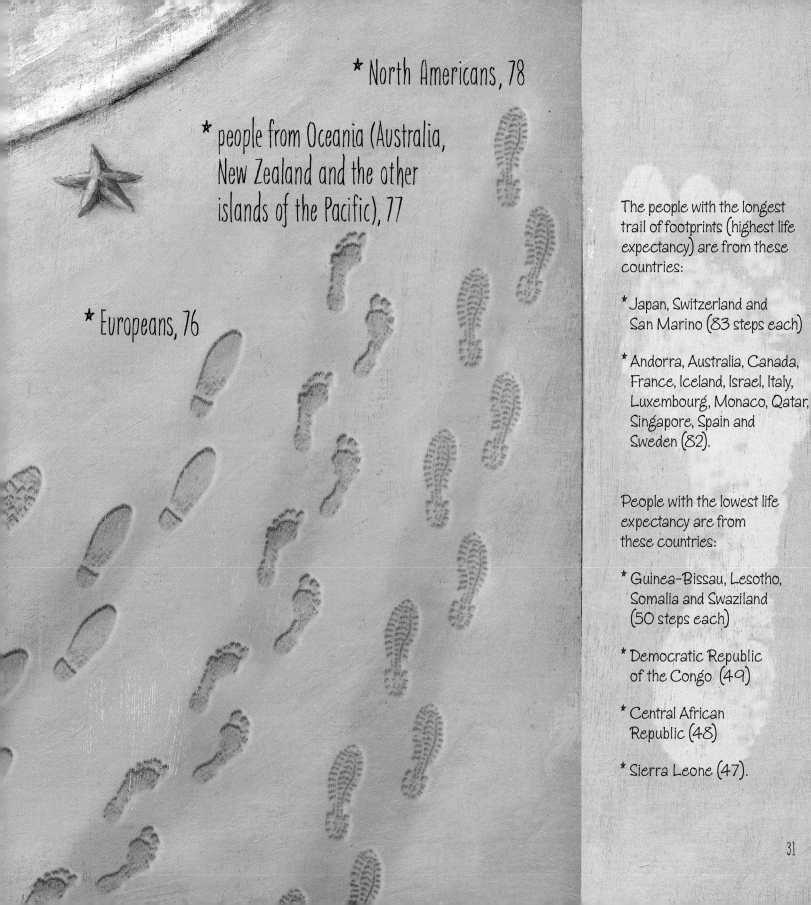

\* North Americans, 78

\* people from Oceania (Australia, New Zealand and the other islands of the Pacific), 77

\* Europeans, 76

The people with the longest trail of footprints (highest life expectancy) are from these countries:

\* Japan, Switzerland and San Marino (83 steps each)

\* Andorra, Australia, Canada, France, Iceland, Israel, Italy, Luxembourg, Monaco, Qatar, Singapore, Spain and Sweden (82).

People with the lowest life expectancy are from these countries:

\* Guinea-Bissau, Lesotho, Somalia and Swaziland (50 steps each)

\* Democratic Republic of the Congo (49)

\* Central African Republic (48)

\* Sierra Leone (47).

# POPULATION

iF today's world population of over 7 billion was represented by a village of 100 people...

* in 1900, there would have been only 32 people in the village because the world's population was much smaller

* in 1800, 17 people

* in 1000 BCE, only 1 person would have lived in the village.

* in 1650, 10 people

* in 1500, 8 people

* in 1 CE, 3 people

Around the world, 15 000 babies are born every hour and 6432 people die. That means in the 10 or so seconds it takes you to read this sentence, 42 babies have been born and 17 people have died, increasing Earth's population by 25 people.

If the world's population keeps growing at its current rate, there will be 129 people in the village by 2050 instead of 100.

# FOOD

**iF** all the food produced around the world in one year was represented by a loaf of bread with 25 slices...

* 11 slices of bread would come from Asia
* 5 from South and Central America
* 4 from Europe
* 2 ¾ from North America
* 2 from Africa
* ¼ from Oceania.

**iF** all the food *consumed* around the world in one year was represented by a loaf of bread with 25 slices...

· 13 ½ slices would be eaten by Asians
· 4 ¼ by Europeans
· 2 ¾ by South and Central Americans
· 2 ½ by Africans
· 1 ¾ by North Americans
· ¼ by people from Oceania (Australia, New Zealand and other islands of the Pacific).

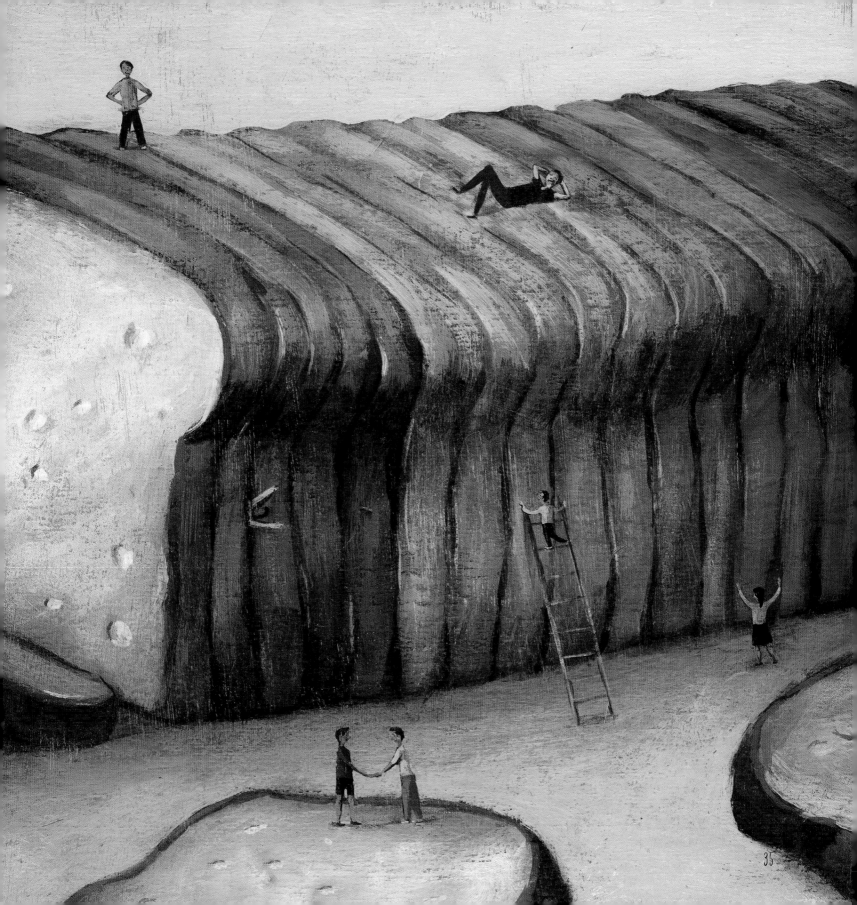

# YOUR LIFE

iF your whole life could
be shown as a jumbo pizza,
divided into 12 slices...

4 slices
would be the time you
spend in school or
at work